Crabtree Publishing Company

www.crabtreebooks.com

Author: Robert Walker
Coordinating editor: Chester Fisher
Series editor: Susan LaBella
Editor: Adrianna Morganelli
Proofreader: Molly Aloian
Editorial director: Kathy Middleton
Production coordinator: Katherine Berti
Prepress technician: Katherine Berti
Project manager: Kumar Kunal (Q2AMEDIA)
Art direction: Rahul Dhiman (Q2AMEDIA)
Cover design: Ritu Chopra (Q2AMEDIA)
Design: Ritu Chopra, Cheena Yadav (Q2AMEDIA)
Photo research: Mariea Janet (Q2AMEDIA)

Photographs:
Alamy: Megapress: p. 31
AP Photo: B. K. Bangash: p. 20; Gurinder Osan: p. 26;
    Lefteris Pitarakis: p. 5; Pavel Rahman: cover
Dreamstime: Aidar Ayazbayev: p. 12; Jeanne Coppens:
    p. 6
Getty Images: John Moore: p. 25; Scott Peterson: p. 28
Masterfile: p. 22
Photolibrary: p. 15, 27; DreamPictures: p. 30
Photos.com: p. 10
Photoshot: Rafael Ben-Ari/Chameleons Eye: p. 27
Reuters: Adrees Latif: p. 13; Daniel Morel: p. 19;
    Pool New: p. 24; Hazir Reka: p. 17; Jayanta Shaw:
    p. 16; Ajay Verma: p. 4
Rex Features: Ilyas J. Dean: p. 1, 23, 29
Shutterstock: p. 7, 9; Ayazad: p. 8; Peter Hansen: p. 11;
    Brett Mulcahy: p. 21; Elzbieta Sekowska: p. 14
World Religions: Christine Osborne Pictures: p. 18

Library and Archives Canada Cataloguing in Publication

Walker, Robert, 1980-
    Eid al-Adha / Robert Walker.

(Celebrations in my world)
Includes index.
ISBN 978-0-7787-4761-1 (bound).--ISBN 978-0-7787-4779-6 (pbk.)

    1. Id al-Adha--Juvenile literature.
I. Title. II. Series: Celebrations in my world

BP186.6.W34 2009   j297.3'6   C2009-905255-5

8487

Library of Congress Cataloging-in-Publication Data

Walker, Robert.
    Eid al-Adha / Robert Walker.
       p. cm. -- (Celebrations in my world)
    Includes index.
    ISBN 978-0-7787-4779-6 (pbk. : alk. paper) -- ISBN 978-0-7787-4761-1
(reinforced library binding : alk. paper)
    1. 'Id al-Adha--Juvenile literature. 2. Fasts and feasts--Islam--Juvenile
literature. 3. Islam--Juvenile literature. I. Title. II. Series.

    BP186.6.W35 2009
    297.3'6--dc22

                                              2009034877

Crabtree Publishing Company

www.crabtreebooks.com   1-800-387-7650

Printed in China/122009/CT20090915

Published in Canada
Crabtree Publishing
616 Welland Ave.
St. Catharines, ON
L2M 5V6

Published in the United States
Crabtree Publishing
350 Fifth Ave.
59th floor
New York, NY 10118

Published in the United Kingdom
Crabtree Publishing
Maritime House
Basin Road North, Hove
BN41 1WR

Published in Australia
Crabtree Publishing
386 Mt. Alexander Rd.
Ascot Vale (Melbourne)
VIC 3032

Contents

What is Eid al-Adha?

Eid al-Adha, or the Festival of **Sacrifice**, is a religious festival celebrated by **Muslims** around the world. Eid al-Adha lasts for several days, depending on where it is being celebrated. It is one of the most important festivals of the Muslim calendar and comes two months after Eid ul-Fitr, the festival that marks the end of Ramadan.

● Muslims during the morning prayer for Eid al-Adha in Chandigarh, India.

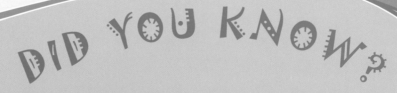

DID YOU KNOW?

Some Muslim businesses close during Eid al-Adha to take part in the celebrations.

Many children dress their best during Eid al-Adha celebrations.

Ramadan is the month when Muslims **fast**. Muslims are people who believe in a religion called **Islam**. During Eid al-Adha celebrations, Muslims wear their best clothes, eat special foods, give gifts, visit with family, and pray at a **mosque**.

Muslims in different countries celebrate Eid al-Adha in their own way.

5

What is Islam?

Islam began in southwestern Asia, in the seventh century. It is based on the teachings of **Muhammad**. Most followers of Islam live in the Middle East, North Africa, and in some parts of Asia. People who believe in Islam obey one God called Allah. They strive to be happy and at peace.

Mosques are places of worship where Muslims come together and pray.

Five times each day, Muslims kneel down and pray in the direction of Mecca, Saudi Arabia, where Muhammad was born.

People of the Islamic faith believe that stealing, disobeying your parents, lying, encouraging slavery, and spreading gossip are sins. Muslims value honesty, respect, and being kind to others.

The Qur'an is a very important book in the Islamic religion. It carries the word of Allah, which all Muslims follow.

DID YOU KNOW?

*The teachings of Islam are collected in a **holy** book called the Qur'an.*

7

Who is Muhammad?

Muhammad was a **prophet** of the Islamic religion and was born in the sixth century. He received messages from Allah, who sent them through the **archangel** Gabriel. Muhammad was visited by Gabriel several times.

Muhammad could not read or write. His followers recorded Allah's messages as Muhammad spoke them.

Muhammad is buried at Medina, Saudi Arabia. Since his death, millions of Muslims have visited his tomb every year.

These teachings then became the holy Qur'an. Muslims believe Muhammad was one of many prophets sent by Allah to spread his teachings. They believe that Muhammad also convinced people who once believed in other gods to worship Allah.

- Muslim children begin learning the history of their faith at a very young age.

DID YOU KNOW?

Many Muslims believe that each person has two special angels who keep track of the good and bad things they do.

9

Origins of Eid al-Adha

Ibrahim is another important Islamic prophet whom Allah sent messages to. Muslims believe Ibrahim was told by Allah to sacrifice his son Isaac, to prove his faith in Allah. Ibrahim agreed to do it. Ibrahim placed his son on an **altar** to sacrifice him to Allah.

At the last moment, Allah replaced Isaac with a ram when it was clear that Ibrahim had proven his **devotion**. Isaac's life was saved.

- Ibrahim was willing to sacrifice his son to prove his faith in Allah.

Today, Muslims celebrate Ibrahim's devotion to Allah during the festival of Eid al-Adha by sacrificing animals.

• Allah gave Ibrahim a ram to sacrifice in place of his son. Today, many Muslims sacrifice a ram for Eid al-Adha.

DID YOU KNOW?

Ibrahim had two sons, Ishmail and Isaac. They both became important people in the Islamic faith.

11

The Hajj

Hajj is a religious pilgrimage, or journey, to Mecca, that millions of Muslims make every year. This is an important trip for Muslims, and is a way for them to show their devotion to the religion of Islam.

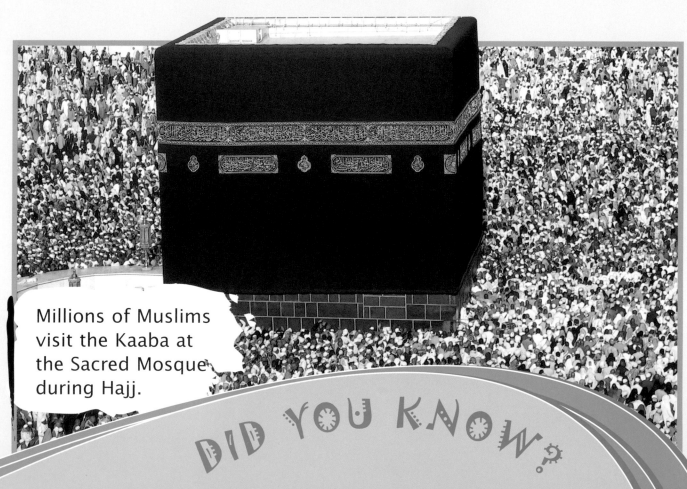

Millions of Muslims visit the Kaaba at the Sacred Mosque during Hajj.

DID YOU KNOW?

In 2008, almost two million people traveled to Saudi Arabia for the Hajj.

During Hajj, Muslims will throw stones at pillars. This honors the story of Ibrahim, who drove away the devil by throwing stones at him.

During the Hajj, Muslims visit several important religious places, including Medina, Mina, the Plain of Arafat, and Muzdaliah. In Mecca, Muslims must walk around the Kaaba. This is a large square building in the middle of the Sacred Mosque. The Kaaba is the most important building in the Islamic religion.

When is Eid al-Adha?

Eid al-Adha is held at the end of Hajj, on the tenth day of the last month of the Muslim calendar. This is a sacred month known as Dhu al-Hijjah.

The Muslim calendar is 11 days shorter than the Gregorian calendar. This means that Eid al-Adha never falls on the same day on the Gregorian calendar. For example, in 2007, Eid al-Adha was held on December 19. In 2008, it was held on December 8.

- The Muslim calendar follows the moon. As the moon's face changes, so do the Muslim months.

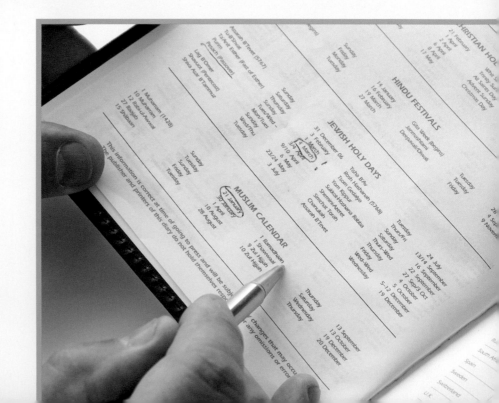

As Eid al-Adha approaches, Muslims start preparing the delicious foods for the festival.

DID YOU KNOW?

Our calendar is called the Gregorian calendar. The Gregorian calendar was introduced by Pope Gregory Xlll in 1582.

15

Eid al-Adha Prayers

Huge crowds of Muslims gather for prayers during Eid al-Adha.

The festival of Eid al-Adha begins with prayer. In the morning, Muslims get up, put on their best clothes, and travel to mosques near their homes. Here, they pray and ask Allah for forgiveness and to help them be better people.

During the festival of Eid al-Adha, Muslims also visit the graves of their friends and family members who have passed on. Muslim families remember and pray for those who have died.

Many Muslims visit the graves of loved ones during Eid al-Adha.

DID YOU KNOW?

Muslims pray five times each day—in the morning, midday, afternoon, at sunset, and in the evening.

Sacrificing an Animal

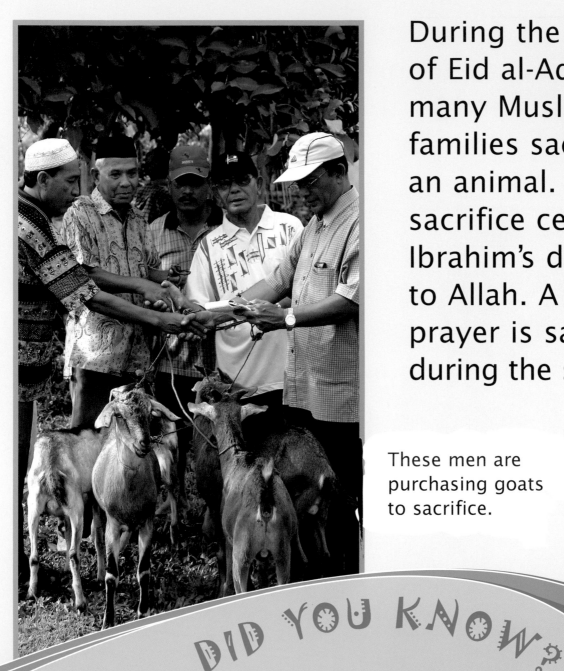

During the festival of Eid al-Adha, many Muslim families sacrifice an animal. This sacrifice celebrates Ibrahim's devotion to Allah. A special prayer is said during the sacrifice.

These men are purchasing goats to sacrifice.

DID YOU KNOW?

Muslims believe that the person who slaughters an animal receives blessings equal to the number of hairs on the animal's body.

This woman is buying her special meat for Eid al-Adha.

Some of the animals used for sacrifice during Eid al-Adha are sheep, goats, cows, and camels. Not all Muslim families in the world sacrifice an animal during the festival of Eid al-Adha.

Instead, they buy special meat from stores that provide it for Muslims during the festival. Muslims who buy their Eid al-Adha meat are still honoring the memory of Ibrahim and his devotion to Allah.

19

The Food

The meat from the sacrificed animals is prepared to be eaten at Eid al-Adha celebrations. Muslims follow Eid al-Adha recipes from around the world.

This family is barbecuing the meat from their sacrificed animal.

DID YOU KNOW?

Some businesses offer to sacrifice the animals for Eid al-Adha.

Muslims eat different kinds of meat during Eid al-Adha, such as lamb, beef, goat, and ram. *Biryani* is a popular dish eaten during Eid al-Adha. It is made with lamb and rice. During the festival, children enjoy sweets such as *vermicelli*, or fine noodle pudding and *sohan halwa*, which is made from semolina, or ground wheat.

This *biryani* dish is made with lamb and rice.

Special Clothing

Everyone is expected to dress their best during Eid al-Adha celebrations. Eid al-Adha is also a time when Muslim children are given gifts of new clothes.

They wear their new clothes to go to parties, **feasts**, and picnics during Eid al-Adha.

- Muslims dress in their finest clothes during the festival.

DID YOU KNOW?

Presents and money are also given to children during Eid al-Adha.

Eid al-Adha is a special time for children. Kids have a lot of fun during the festival.

Adults also wear their best clothes during Eid al-Adha celebrations. Male Muslims often wear jackets, tunics, or a *galabiyya*, or long shirt.

Muslim females dress in their best blouses, tunics, long dresses, and *hijab*, or head scarf.

23

Giving to the Needy

Iraqi Prime Minister Iyad Allawi hands out presents to orphans during Eid al-Adha.

Muslims make special efforts to be sure that no one is without sacrificial food during Eid al-Adha.

DID YOU KNOW?

An animal chosen for sacrifice during Eid al-Adha must be healthy, and of a certain age.

Each family gives part of the meat from their sacrificed animal to those who cannot afford the meat themselves. Charity is an important part of the Islamic faith.

In places where Muslims do not sacrifice animals, they make donations to charities that provide sacrificial meat to others during Eid al-Adha celebrations. Many Muslims also give money to those in need during Eid al-Adha.

No one goes without sacrificial meat during the festival. Muslims donate food to those in need during Eid al-Adha.

25

Friends and Family

Many Muslims visit with friends and family during Eid al-Adha. They hug and exchange greetings and celebrate Eid al-Adha together. It is a special time for families.

Muslims celebrate Eid al-Adha with friends and family.

DID YOU KNOW?

Eid al-Adha is only one of the festivals introduced by Muhammad. Another is Eid ul-Fitr, which means "to break the fast."

Sharing food is an important part of Eid al-Adha.

During Eid al-Adha celebrations, families give thanks for the food they have. They share the foods made special for the festival, as well as the meat from their sacrificed animals.

Muslim adults exchange presents with one another, as well as with the children.

A Worldwide Holiday

Depending where they live, Muslims celebrate Eid al-Adha differently. In some places, Muslim families have picnics or go to amusement parks during the festival. For some Muslims, a big part of Eid al-Adha is going to places and doing things that children will enjoy.

A Muslim girl enjoys a ride at an amusement park.

DID YOU KNOW?

In Turkey, the festival of Eid al-Adha is known as Kurban Bayrami.

Some followers of Islam enjoy singing and dancing during Eid al-Adha celebrations. Special concerts are held to entertain Muslim crowds with music and other events.

Muslims from Pakistan dance to Eid al-Adha music.

Islam Worldwide

The Islamic religion has spread to different countries all over the world.

The whole Muslim world is called *Ummah*. It is made up of people who are connected by their shared belief in Islam.

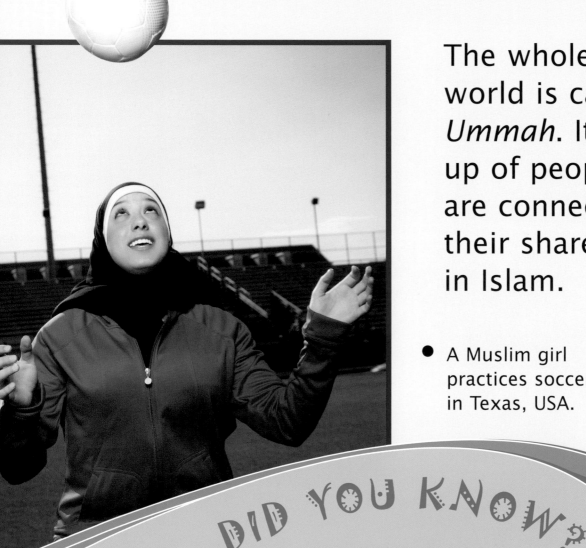

- A Muslim girl practices soccer in Texas, USA.

DID YOU KNOW?

According to the Qur'an, Muslim women are supposed to wear robes that cover their whole bodies when they leave the house. This shows their devotion to the Islamic faith.

In some middle eastern countries, Muslims make up the majority of the people living there. Muslims also live in other countries around the world.

Islam is one of the fastest-growing religions in the world. More and more people are **converting**, or joining, Islam every day.

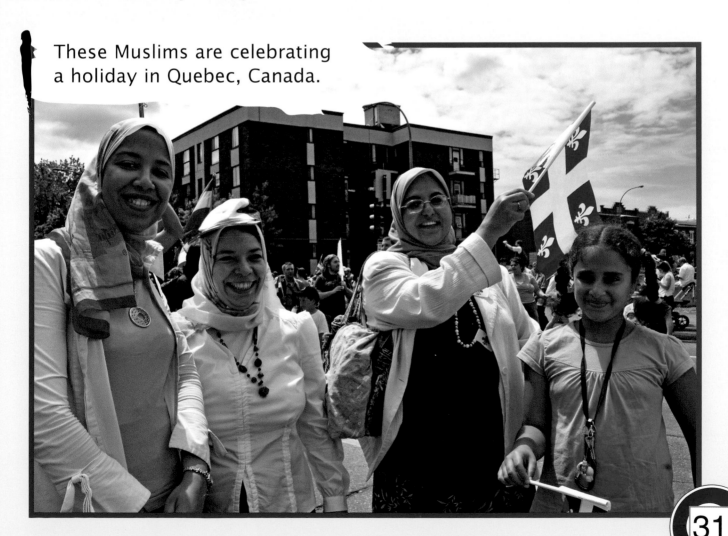

These Muslims are celebrating a holiday in Quebec, Canada.

Glossary

altar A flat surface used for religious practices

archangel The most important and highest-ranking angel

converting Changing of religion or belief

devotion Loyalty or belief

fast To not eat

feast A big meal

holy Important to a religion

Islam A Muslim religion

mosque A building where Muslims go to pray

Muhammad A prophet of the Islamic religion

Muslim A follower of Islam

prophet The messenger of God (Allah)

sacrifice Killing an animal, usually for a religious reason

Index